6.2/1.

SEP

2004

MW01009675

Mount Vernon

by Andrew Santella

Content Adviser: Mary V. Thompson, Research Specialist,
Mount Vernon Ladies' Association,
Mount Vernon, Virginia

Reading Adviser: Rosemary G. Palmer, Ph.D.,
Department of Literacy, College of Education,
Boise State University

COMPASS POINT BOOKS
MINNEAPOLIS, MINNESOTA

Compass Point Books
3109 West 50th Street, #115
Minneapolis, MN 55410

Visit Compass Point Books on the Internet at *www.compasspointbooks.com*
or e-mail your request to *custserv@compasspointbooks.com*

On the cover: Mount Vernon, George Washington's home

Photographs ©: Declan McCullah, cover; Ted Spiegel/Corbis, 4, 17, 20; North Wind Picture
Archives, 5, 12, 21; Courtesy of the Mount Vernon Ladies' Association, 6, 10, 14, 26, 28; Library
of Congress, 7, 19, 27, 36; N. Carter/North Wind Picture Archives, 8, 24, 29, 30, 32; Todd A.
Gipstein/Corbis, 9, 15, 23; Hulton/Archive by Getty Images, 11; Wolfgang Kaehler/Corbis, 13;
Historical Picture Archive/Corbis, 16; Peter Finger/Corbis, 18; Kevin Fleming/Corbis, 22; Deirdre
Barton, 31; Robert Knopes/Omni-Photo Communications, 33; Reuters NewMedia Inc./Corbis, 34;
The Corcoran Gallery of Art/Corbis, 35; Stock Montage, Inc., 37; Bettmann/Corbis, 38, 39; James
P. Blair/Corbis, 41.

Creative Director: Terri Foley
Managing Editor: Catherine Neitge
Photo Researcher: Marcie C. Spence
Designer/Page production: Bradfordesign, Inc./Jaime Martens
Cartographer: XNR Productions, Inc.

Library of Congress Cataloging-in-Publication Data
Santella, Andrew.
  Mount Vernon / by Andrew Santella.
     p. cm. — (We the people)
Includes bibliographical references (p.) and index.
  ISBN 0-7565-0682-4 (hardcover)
 1. Mount Vernon (Va. : Estate)—Juvenile literature. 2. Washington, George, 1732-1799—Homes
and haunts—Virginia—Fairfax County—Juvenile literature. [1. Mount Vernon (Va.: Estate)
2. Washington, George, 1732-1799—Homes and haunts.] I. Title. II. We the people (Series)
(Compass Point Books)
E312.5.S18 2004
973.4'1'092—dc22   2003024189

TABLE OF CONTENTS

NOTE: *In this book, words that are defined in the glossary are in* **bold** *the first time they appear in the text.*

HAPPY AT HOME

In 1754, a young man named George Washington became master of a large **estate** on the banks of the Potomac River in Virginia. The estate was called Mount Vernon, and Washington would live there for the rest of his adult life.

Washington was just 22 years old when he became master of Mount Vernon. He had not yet begun the career that would win him lasting fame all around the world.

Winter at Mount Vernon, George Washington's home for many years

General George Washington in 1783, near the end of the Revolutionary War

In the years to come, Washington would command the Continental Army in its fight against Britain to win independence for the United States. He would preside over the Constitutional Convention of 1787 to create a new system of government for the young country. Then from 1789 to 1797, he would serve as the first president of the United States.

This portrait of George and Martha Washington and grandchildren was painted in 1796. An original 1798 engraving of it hangs at Mount Vernon.

Time after time, Washington was called on to serve his country. Yet he always returned to his home at Mount Vernon. He lived there for 45 years. In 1759, he brought his bride Martha, who was a widow, and her two children, John and Martha, to live there with him. Later, two of Martha's grandchildren would live with them as well.

Washington often told his friends that he was happiest when he was at home. He once wrote: "I can truly say I had rather be at home at Mount Vernon with a friend or two about me than to be attended at the seat of government by the officers of state and the representatives of every power in Europe."

A VISIT TO MOUNT VERNON

Each year, hundreds of people visited Mount Vernon to meet its famous master and admire his handsome estate. Friends and relatives came to visit, of course.

However, passing travelers often stopped at Mount Vernon without invitations. Martha Washington sometimes gave visitors a tour of the house. Some stayed for dinner, and others were even invited to stay overnight. Washington once observed that his house was like "a well-resorted tavern,"

George Washington and family say goodbye to a guest, General Lafayette.

because so many travelers going from north to south or from south to north made a point of staying there for at least a day or two.

Riding up to the house on horseback or in a carriage, visitors followed a long and winding driveway around a wide lawn and up to the front door. High atop the roof of the house sat a weather vane depicting a dove carrying an olive branch. It was placed to celebrate the end of the Revolutionary War, as a symbol of peace.

Mount Vernon's dove weather vane symbolizes peace.

Mount Vernon overlooks the Potomac River in northern Virginia.

Other visitors traveled to Mount Vernon by water. Boats could dock on the shores of the Potomac River just below Washington's house. The house towered about 125 feet (38 meters) above the river on a high bank. From its beautiful **piazza** visitors could enjoy stunning views of the river and shoreline.

9

Washington depended on slaves, many of whom lived in the communal quarters of the center brick building. They also lived in parts of the greenhouse at the right.

Mount Vernon was more than Washington's home. It was also his principal business. Today, Washington is remembered as a soldier and a **statesman.** He thought of himself, however, as a farmer. At Mount Vernon, he grew wheat and other crops, using the most advanced farming techniques of his era. He also ran other thriving businesses there, including a **fishery** and a flour mill.

Washington was a successful businessman, but his success depended on the hard work of the slaves at Mount

Vernon. In the last years of Washington's life, more than 300 slaves worked for him. They performed all the most difficult and most dangerous jobs. Washington may have run things at Mount Vernon, but slaves did the daily work. Without them, the plantation could not have flourished.

George Washington watches as slaves work at Mount Vernon.

The land that Mount Vernon occupies had been owned by the Washington family since 1674. It was George Washington's older half-brother Lawrence who named the property Mount Vernon. The name honors Admiral Edward Vernon, who was Lawrence's commander in the British Navy. Much of George Washington's teenage

Lawrence Washington

years were spent living with Lawrence at Mount Vernon.

After Lawrence died in 1752, George arranged to lease Mount Vernon from Lawrence's widow, Anne. When Anne died in 1761, George inherited Mount Vernon and became its owner.

12

From the start, George Washington loved Mount Vernon. "No estate in United America is more pleasantly situated than this," he once wrote. "It lies in a high, dry and healthy country, three hundred miles by water from the sea, and ... on one of the finest rivers in the land." Washington worked almost continually to improve Mount Vernon until the day he died.

The Potomac River can be seen through Mount Vernon's covered walkway.

IMPROVING MOUNT VERNON

When George Washington took over Mount Vernon, the main building was a simple four-room farmhouse. One of his first projects was rebuilding that house. Washington added a whole new level of rooms, raising the house to two-and-a-half stories. He also redecorated the rooms inside. He ordered expensive wallpaper and oil paintings from England. He had workmen carve fancy designs into

A reconstruction of the elaborate greenhouse, which was destroyed in an 1835 fire

Mount Vernon's wooden clapboards resemble blocks of stone.

the wood trim around doors and fireplaces. In the main entrance to the house, he had fine wood paneling installed.

Washington made improvements to the outside of the house as well. The outside walls were made of wooden **clapboards,** but they were treated to look like stone. To accomplish this, the wooden boards were first carved into rectangles, so they resembled blocks of stone stacked on top of each other. Then they were covered with several alternating layers of white paint and sand. The sand was applied while the paint was still wet so that it would stick. The effect was to give the wood the look of stone.

From a distance, the walls did indeed resemble stone. Only if a visitor knocked on the walls would it become clear that they were really made of wood.

Work on the house went slowly. One room took 12 years to finish. Many of the materials had to be ordered from England, and workmen often had to wait months for the materials they needed to complete a job. In fact, Washington made so many improvements to Mount Vernon that work

A hand-colored print of the completed Mount Vernon was published in the early 1800s.

on the house hardly ever stopped. Washington and his family had to get used to living surrounded by painters and carpenters for years at a time. The sound of hammers rapping and the smell of paint were most likely part of living at Mount Vernon.

George Washington chose trees to make the grounds look their best.

Washington also worked to make the grounds of the estate look their best. He designed the gardens and walkways that went around the outside of the house. He personally picked the trees that were planted around the driveway leading to the house. Some of those trees still stand today.

Washington designed the gardens at Mount Vernon.

The biggest change Washington made was in the size of the estate. Over the years, he kept buying more land in the area and adding to his holdings. When he first became owner, Mount Vernon was an estate of about 2,000 acres (800 hectares). As Washington bought more land, Mount Vernon grew to include about 8,000 acres (3,200 hectares).

18

GEORGE WASHINGTON, FARMER

Washington liked to wake early at Mount Vernon, often before sunrise. That meant the servants and cooks of Mount Vernon had to wake early as well. By the time Washington finished washing and shaving, they had to have his breakfast ready. He especially liked cornmeal pancakes with butter and honey. After breakfast, Washington might go to his private study and write letters. He also loved to take one of his horses for a ride around

Washington checked on the work at Mount Vernon on horseback.

Mount Vernon. He kept more than 20 horses and used them to visit the different parts of his huge plantation. Washington liked to personally look over the work being done in his farm fields.

He usually returned to the house in time for dinner at 3 P.M. To people today, the dinners at Mount Vernon might sound enormous, but they were pretty typical for people like the Washingtons in the 18th century. One visitor remembered a Mount Vernon dinner that included boiled pork, goose, roast beef, corned beef, mutton chops, hominy,

A dining table at Mount Vernon displays a re-creation of a meal described in one of George Washington's journals.

20

cabbage, potatoes, pickles, and onions. For dessert, there were pies, tarts, and cheeses, followed by a final course of apples, two kinds of nuts, raisins, and sweet wines. Conversation between the Washingtons and their guests was usually about farming or current events.

George Washington loved farming.

Farming, in fact, was one of Washington's favorite topics. He was proud to consider himself a farmer, and he thought it was one of the finest occupations in the world. "It is honorable. It is amusing, and, with judicious management, it is profitable," he once wrote of farming.

When Washington began farming at Mount Vernon, he grew mostly tobacco. In fact, tobacco was the main crop of most Virginia plantations of that time.

However, he soon came to believe that growing tobacco was bad for his farming business. He saw that planting tobacco year after year quickly drained the soil of the nutrients that plants need to grow. Washington also did not like depending on English agents to sell his tobacco overseas. He suspected those agents cheated him out of profits.

22

Tobacco robbed the Mount Vernon soil of nutrients.

So in the 1760s, Washington switched from growing tobacco as his main crop to growing mostly wheat. It was easier to produce, and wheat was easier on the Mount Vernon soil. Washington proved to be ahead of his time

Wheat grown at Mount Vernon has been loaded into a cart.

in switching to wheat. Before long, most other planters in the area followed his lead and began growing wheat instead of tobacco.

The switch to wheat helped to make the Mount Vernon plantation more profitable. Washington also looked for ways to improve the soil there. He successfully used a system of farming called crop rotation. Washington knew that planting only one crop in the same fields, season after season, tended to wear out the soil and eventually produced poorer harvests. Some farmers in Virginia simply planted one kind of crop, such as tobacco, over and over until they could no longer produce good harvests. Then they would abandon their farms and move onto new land.

A tilled field at present-day Mount Vernon

Washington and other farmers took another approach. They began rotating their crops. In other words, Washington began planting different crops in different fields each year to preserve the quality of his soil. For example, after growing wheat in one field one year, he would grow corn or potatoes in that field the following year. In addition, he let fields lay **fallow** every few years and planted nothing but grass or clover for livestock to feed on. This system helped the soil restore itself and regain the nutrients needed for successful harvests.

THE SLAVES OF MOUNT VERNON

Washington's estate was so large that he divided it into five separate farms. Each farm had its own storage buildings and its own workforce of slaves. At each farm, the slaves worked under the watchful eye of an **overseer.** The overseer's job was to keep the slaves working efficiently.

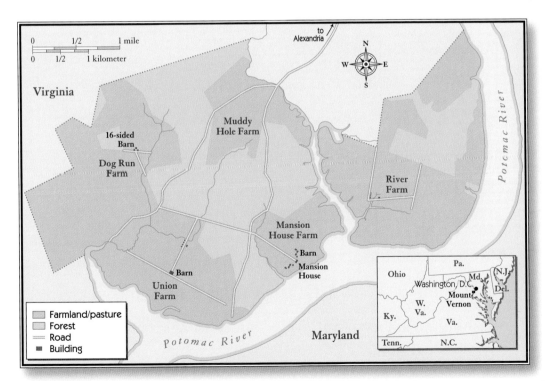

Mount Vernon was divided into five farms.

A reconstruction of the Mansion House slave quarters

Some overseers punished slaves harshly if they failed to do their work.

When Washington became master of Mount Vernon, he began adding to his workforce of slaves. He bought slaves at public auctions and inherited slaves from relatives. In 1760, there were 43 adult slaves living at Mount Vernon. By 1799, more than 300 slaves lived and worked there. Most were field hands, or workers who tended to the crops on Washington's farms. Others worked as servants in Washington's house. Still others worked at specialized jobs such as cooking or carpentry.

Washington considered himself a farmer, but it was Mount Vernon's field hands who did the hard work that made crops grow. As Washington bought more and more land, they cleared it and made it ready for planting. They removed rocks and boulders and dug up large tree stumps. They plowed, planted, and weeded. They built fences around the fields. Work began at sunrise and lasted until sunset, with two hours off for meal breaks. Mothers working in the fields probably took their infants with them. By the time a child turned 11 or 12, he or she was put to work, too.

An oil painting by Junius Brutus Stearns shows Washington and his farm slaves.

None of Mount Vernon's slave quarters are still standing today, but this early 20th-century photo is believed to be of a slave cabin.

Field hands lived in small huts made of logs and clay, with dirt floors. A visitor from Poland was shocked at the living conditions of Mount Vernon slaves. He wrote that the slaves' cabins were "more miserable than the most miserable of the cottages of our peasants." Each family or group of slaves was given one week's supply of food at a time. They were also allowed to keep small gardens where they could grow fruits and vegetables. Some raised chickens.

Slaves kept Mount Vernon working. Yet Washington sometimes wrote of his desire to give the slaves of Mount Vernon their freedom. "There is not a man living who wishes more sincerely than I do, to see a plan adopted for the abolition of [slavery]," he wrote in 1786. As long as Washington lived, however, he continued to depend on the labor of enslaved people at Mount Vernon.

In his will, he made arrangements to free the slaves that he owned. After Washington's death, 123 of Mount Vernon's slaves were freed. After Martha Washington died, 153 of the slaves were divided among her four grandchildren. Another 40 slaves had been rented from a neighbor and were returned to their owner. George Washington made arrangements in his will to provide an education for the younger slaves who were being freed and to provide care for his former slaves who were elderly.

A memorial stands in the slave burial ground at Mount Vernon.

MOUNT VERNON BUSINESSES

Washington was always looking for ways to make his farms and other businesses work better. He was willing to try unusual ideas, such as the new barn he built for **treading** wheat. At most farms, workers hit stalks of wheat with sticks, called flails, to separate the useful grain from the stalk. Washington's barn was designed to make **threshing** wheat easier and faster.

Though it appeared to be round, the barn was really 16-sided. It was divided into an upper level and a lower level.

Washington's treading barn has 16 sides.

The floor on the upper level was built with gaps between the wooden boards. At threshing time, wheat was spread on the floor of the upper level. Then horses trotted around and around on top of the wheat, separating the grain from the stalks. The grain then fell through the gaps in the floor to the lower level, where it was collected and stored.

Washington believed mules were good for farmwork and used many at Mount Vernon.

Washington is also given credit for promoting the use of mules on American farms. Washington loved horses, but he believed that mules were stronger and easier to care for than horses—and that they were better suited for farmwork. While most farmers relied on horses,

Washington depended more and more on mules. By the end of his life, there were 57 mules at Mount Vernon.

Not all of Washington's ideas worked so well. He often complained about the expense and labor of building and repairing fences on his farms. Fences were necessary to keep livestock and other animals out of the farm fields, but they always seemed to need mending. Washington tried to replace some of his man-made fences with "natural fences" of trees and bushes. He planted young seedlings and shrubs in rows along the

Fences surround Mount Vernon's vegetable gardens.

Washington's mill for grinding wheat and corn has been rebuilt and can be toured.

edges of fields, hoping they would grow to form a barrier that would keep animals out. However, the new plants never seemed to survive very long, so natural fences never replaced man-made ones at Mount Vernon.

Washington started several moneymaking businesses at Mount Vernon. He built a mill for grinding wheat and corn into flour and meal. The mill was driven by water from a creek that flowed through Washington's property. It processed wheat from Mount Vernon and neighboring farms. Washington even started selling his own brand of flour in Virginia and other nearby areas.

Archaeologists are excavating Washington's distillery, which will be rebuilt.

Not far from the mill, he started a distillery. The whiskey produced there turned out to be an excellent source of profits for Washington.

Another success was the fishery at Mount Vernon. Taking advantage of the plentiful fish in the Potomac River, workers harvested huge catches each year. One year, Washington's workers were said to have caught 1 million fish in six weeks. The fish were salted to preserve them, then placed in large barrels. Some were used at the plantation, others were sold at markets in America and the West Indies.

Washington's years serving his country as a soldier and a statesman kept him away from home for long stretches of time. During the Revolutionary War, he went six years without a visit to his beloved Mount Vernon. When he served as president, the nation's capital was New York City and then Philadelphia. The long journey from the capital to Mount Vernon could take more than a week on horseback, so Washington could not come home as often as he would have liked when he was president.

Washington enjoyed his final years in retirement at Mount Vernon. "At length, I am become a private citizen on the bank of the Potomac," he wrote happily late in his life.

Rembrandt Peele painted this famous work showing Washington on horseback.

Finally, he was able to devote his full attention to his home and his farms. On December 12, 1799, while taking one of his usual horseback tours of his farms, he was caught in a sudden storm of rain, hail, and snow. His overcoat kept him dry, except for his head and neck. The next morning, he woke with a sore throat, but he still went out in a heavy snowfall to mark some trees for cutting. In the middle of the night, his condition suddenly worsened.

Washington died on the evening of December 14, 1799, at age 67. He is buried at Mount Vernon. The inscription above his tomb reads, "Within this Enclosure Rest the remains of Genl. George Washington."

This 1850 image shows George Washington's tomb.

SAVING MOUNT VERNON

After George Washington's death, Martha Washington continued to live at Mount Vernon. She would not go back into either the room she and her husband once shared or Washington's study, however, so she moved upstairs to a smaller room. She died at Mount Vernon in 1802.

Martha Washington

Washington's nephew Bushrod took over ownership of Mount Vernon, but he lived there just a few months each year. He was not as skillful, or as interested, in farming as his uncle had been. Bushrod was busy as a justice of the United States Supreme Court and as an executor of George Washington's estate. He had to take care of the newly freed elderly slaves from Mount Vernon until they died.

37

Within a few decades, the house needed serious repairs. The roof was near collapse. Legend has it that old ships' masts were used to prop up Washington's beautiful old piazza. Visitors continued to come to look at Washington's old home, but now they left disturbed by its poor condition.

The last member of the Washington family to own Mount Vernon was John Augustine Washington III, the great-grandnephew of George Washington. He was

Mount Vernon's lovely piazza showed no signs of once being propped up by masts when President and Mrs. John Kennedy hosted a dinner there in 1961 for the president of Pakistan and his daughter.

38

This photo of Mount Vernon was taken in 1858 before it was renovated.

unable to afford the expensive repairs that Mount Vernon needed, so he hoped to sell the estate. He offered to sell Mount Vernon to either the state of Virginia or to the United States government, but neither would come forward with the money to buy it.

Then in 1853, a woman named Ann Pamela Cunningham learned of the crisis at Mount Vernon. Cunningham's mother had cruised past Mount Vernon on a boat trip down the Potomac River and was saddened by the house's condition. When she told her daughter about the old house, Ann vowed to do something to help. She organized a group of women from all over the country to raise money to buy Mount Vernon. Their goal was to save the house and preserve it as a national treasure. They called themselves the Mount Vernon Ladies' Association of the Union. Today, they are considered by many to be the first national organization devoted to the preservation of a historic site.

For five years, Cunningham and her group worked to convince John Augustine Washington III to sell to a group of women. Between 1858 and 1860, they raised $200,000 to purchase Washington's house and 200 acres (80 hectares) of the original estate. The Mount Vernon Ladies' Association acquired the property in 1860 and vowed to return the house to the way it looked at the time of Washington's death.

The association continues to own and run the estate today. Over the years, it has restored the house to look as much as possible as it did in 1799. Experts have worked to closely reproduce even the color of the paint used in the house. Much of Washington's original furniture has been purchased and returned to the house.

40

Other parts of Mount Vernon have been restored to their original condition as well. Visitors can see a re-creation of Washington's 16-sided barn and get a demonstration of how it worked. They can visit an example of slave quarters at Mount Vernon and get a glimpse of everyday life on an 18th-century plantation. Just as it was in Washington's day, Mount Vernon remains a popular attraction for visitors. About 1 million people visit each year to see and experience the home that George Washington loved.

Mount Vernon remains a popular tourist attraction.

GLOSSARY

clapboards—narrow boards used for siding

estate—a large piece of land, usually with a large house on it

fallow—left unplanted for a season

fishery—place where fish are caught and prepared for sale

overseer—one who keeps watch over and directs the work of others, especially slaves or laborers

piazza—a large, open porch

statesman—a wise political leader

threshing—to beat crops to separate the grain from the rest of the crop

treading—the trampling of wheat by horses to separate the grain from the rest of the crop

42

DID YOU KNOW?

- During the Revolutionary War (1775-1783), George Washington spent only about 10 days at his beloved Mount Vernon. He stopped there on his way to and from the Battle of Yorktown in 1781.

- George Washington took no salary in return for his services as commander in chief of the Continental Army during the Revolutionary War.

- Martha Washington was a skilled seamstress and sewed seat cushions and other items for Mount Vernon.

IMPORTANT DATES

Timeline

1674	George Washington's great grandfather, John Washington, is granted ownership of land that will become Mount Vernon.
1732	George Washington is born on February 22.
1752	George Washington's older half-brother, Lawrence Washington, dies.
1754	George Washington begins leasing Mount Vernon.
1759	George Washington marries a young widow, Martha Dandridge Custis, who has two children.
1761	George Washington inherits Mount Vernon.
1775–1783	Washington commands the Continental Army in the Revolutionary War.
1789–1797	George Washington serves as president.
1799	George Washington dies on December 14.
1802	Martha Washington dies on May 22.
1853	Ann Pamela Cunningham founds the Mount Vernon Ladies' Association of the Union.
1858	Mount Vernon Ladies' Association begins raising funds to buy Mount Vernon.
1860	Mount Vernon Ladies' Association takes over Mount Vernon.

IMPORTANT PEOPLE

ANN PAMELA CUNNINGHAM (1816–1875)

Founder of the Mount Vernon Ladies' Association of the Union who led the campaign to purchase Mount Vernon and preserve it as a historic site

GEORGE WASHINGTON (1732–1799)

Master of Mount Vernon who was commander of the Continental Army during the Revolutionary War and the first president of the United States

LAWRENCE WASHINGTON (ca. 1718–1752)

Older half-brother of George Washington who lived at Mount Vernon from 1743 until his death in 1752

MARTHA WASHINGTON (1731–1802)

Widow who married George Washington in 1759 and became mistress of Mount Vernon; Martha and George Washington raised her two children from her previous marriage and two of her grandchildren at Mount Vernon.

WANT TO KNOW MORE?

At the Library

Burgan, Michael. *George Washington.* Minneapolis: Compass Point
Books, 2003.

Collins, Mary. *Mount Vernon.* New York: Children's Press, 1998.

Marrin, Albert. *George Washington and the Founding of a Nation.*
New York: Dutton Children's Books, 2001.

On the Web

For more information on *Mount Vernon,* use FactHound

to track down Web sites related to this book.

1. Go to *www.facthound.com*

2. Type in a search word related to this book
   or this book ID: 0756506824.

3. Click on the *Fetch It* button.

Your trusty FactHound will fetch the best Web sites for you!

On the Road

Historic Mount Vernon

3200 Mount Vernon Memorial Highway

Mount Vernon, VA 22121

703/780-2000

To visit George Washington's house and gardens

INDEX

About the Author

Andrew Santella writes for magazines and newspapers, including *GQ* and the *New York Times Book Review*. He is the author of a number of books for young readers. He lives outside Chicago with his wife and son.